Coping With Kids

A simple book to help anyone who looks after children

Jon Martin & Mick Rose

FOREWORD

Jon and Mick have crafted an excellent little book of very empowering tips for children, parents, grandparents and anyone involved in the care of young people. As an experienced teacher in the NLP community, I am humbled by their insightful wisdom which certainly will enhance my skills as a grandparent. Coping with Kids is packed with the essentials of NLP based on the authors' hands-on application in therapy and parenting. This highly readable booklet will change attitudes to childcare.

Dr Susi Strang Wood, Master Trainer of NLP, UKCP Registered Psychotherapist

Contents

	Page number
Foreword	1
Contents	2
Childhood and common problems	3
Chunking information	4
Get into their world & What if you did know?	5
Memory skills	6
Dealing with worries & Giving responsibility	7
Building resilience	8
Ignore them!	11
Look for what you want	12
Draw away the problems	13
How to build confidence	14
Do something nice & We wanna be together	17
What if? & Use your senses	18
Nightmares	19
Actions speak louder	20
Use the skills of someone who can & Focus on what you want	21
And sleeeeeep! & Anchor positive behaviour	22
Eye movements	23
The dentist!	24
The power of story telling & Little Nicky	25
The Authors	27

(C) Hednesford Publications 2014

Childhood

Childhood should be a happy, carefree time, full of love and laughter. Children, like adults, face challenges in every-day life and sometimes find it hard to make sense of their experiences and feelings. These experiences can have a negative impact on the child's behaviour now and in the future.

It's extremely important for a child to have the opportunity to understand their feelings and emotions. Doing so will lead to them growing up equipped to achieve their full potential.

Common problems for children include

exam/school worries
lack of confidence
motivation
phobias
bereavement
family break-up
irregular sleep patterns
emotional & behavioural difficulties

Children interact and respond more easily than grown-ups because their minds are open to the idea of improvement. It's a natural human condition to want to improve, learn and develop. Kids have not yet received the same conditioning from life that adults have, which means that really positive results can occur much quicker when working with children.

We're going to give you 20 or so really powerful tips (and some fantastic case studies) for helping kids to develop, all of which will also make your life easier too.

Chunk information to make it easier to understand

Chunking is a way of measuring information. When information is global we have the overall view of everything there is to know, the "bigger picture". When information is specific, we have the details. Some children find global information a bit too much to take in and become overwhelmed, their confusion leading to inaction. To prevent this from happening, present information to children in smaller chunks or in very specific steps without overwhelming them with the overall big picture.

For example, ask a child to tidy their bookshelf. Then when that is done, ask them to put their clothes away. This use of small specific steps is less demanding than the big picture order to "go and tidy your whole room." Giving the information in small steps makes it much more achievable, plus you have the added bonus of being able to give feedback on their progress as they go along which will be much more encouraging to them.

It's the same when you're asking questions. Have you ever asked...."How was your day at school?"......to be met by an indifferent shrug. Reason? – it's just too much stuff! What did Mrs Jones say today? How did you get on with Matthew? I bet you had fun at playtime? Who was your best friend today? A bunch of little chunk questions in a conversational manner will elicit more information than any amount of big picture thinking.

Get into their world

There's a long held view that in order to get into rapport with another person, you have to "get into their world". It's true to say that you don't make friends by talking about yourself and kids are no different. Find a common interest and talk about it. Subtly match their body language, even if this feels strange. This will enable you to gain rapport and then you'll be able to enter a conversation that has previously eluded you. Kids adopt funny postures sometimes – do the same. Even use a few of their words and phrases back to them and see how they warm to you, really quickly.

As they gain confidence and share their thoughts, pace and lead them into new behaviours. You can do this quite easily by saying....."I bet you were angry when that happened?......followed by......"Being angry is horrible though isn't it?"........and adopting a different body shape as you say so. You can re-enforce this by adding......" So what makes you happy then?".......and watch how the child's attitude and behaviour transform quickly.

Also - from this conversation you can elicit their likes and dislikes and find out what makes them tick.

What if you did know??

Children will often say "I don't know" to keep them from thinking or dealing with a difficult situation. Or they may be too lazy to use their brain. Ask them..........."what if you did know?"............this changes the child's way of thinking and also empowers them to think! Explore variations of this. "What's your favourite colour?"................." don't know!".............."what would it be if you did know?"

Memory skills using association

A good technique to help children learn more and retain information is to use association. Turning your important content and information (such as stuff that needs to be remembered for tests) into crazy stories will help it stick in the child's mind more effectively. The more bizarre the story, the better it will stick. For example, instead of remembering a list of words, such as candle, phone, alien, bed, sick, bottle, fruit machine, candy and box, you can get them to visualise the following story. Remembering the exact wording of the story isn't important.

"There once was a little yellow candle that came to life (like the one in beauty and the beast). It picked up the telephone and on the other end was an alien who said it was in bed and couldn't get up because he was feeling sick. He said he had drunk a whole bottle of red medicine and was now feeling sick and his skin had turned purple. He had got sick after spending all his money at the fruit machine, and had won lots of candy. He'd eaten the lot and was now being sick in a wooden toy box."

Remembering the visual images and the content of the strange story is much easier than just remembering a list of words.

Dealing with worries

Something that can work well in helping children with the transitions they experience in life (such as changing schools, moving house, or a family bereavement) is to install a "worry box." Children write their concerns on a piece of paper and post them in the box. Just the process of doing this can help to take the weight off their shoulders and also offers you the opportunity to address them in a more covert and subtle way, issues that you might not otherwise have been aware of.

Giving responsibility

Jon once worked with a child who had some challenges with eating. When he met her she said that she never ate at school even though she was hungry. As soon as she arrived at the canteen she lost her appetite. Jon asked if she knew what might cause this and she said she felt it was because the canteen wasn't always clean or comfortable. It turns out she is quite a fussy eater at home too. Jon suggested that she become more involved in cooking her meals (to help her feel a bit more in control of what she is eating) and about 15 minutes later she suddenly exclaimed "I could make my own lunch too! And maybe have pasta instead of sandwiches all the time. Or a bun, or a wrap. I could even have more vegetables and put them in my lunch!"

Consider where you can give children more responsibility in their life. If you can make it seem like an exciting treat to do something that is normally reserved for grown-ups (rather than something you hate doing and want to off-load to them) they'll be really keen to do it. Wherever you give them more responsibility, you give them more power and this is especially useful in areas where they are facing challenges.

Case Study #1 – Building Resilience in Children

Ever been to a "Go Ape" venue? Read on:

And so it was, on a family holiday in the South of France last year, that along with my eldest daughter (Imogen, aged 10), I found myself clinging to a tree for dear life, 15 metres up, streaming with sweat and wondering why I'd paid good money to put us through such a trial. Unfortunately for Imogen's two cousins (also aged 10), they were up there with us, hanging on and also wishing they were back on solid ground.

Now there are a lot of similarities between my daughter and her cousins. They're all sporty, fit, happy and outgoing, they receive strong parenting and are encouraged greatly in the various aspects of their lives, but on that day, there was one crucial difference between them which meant that Imogen completed the course while her cousins had to be helped down by the staff and went home disappointed that they'd not been able to complete it.

Due to some of the unique challenges which Imogen has faced as a child, she's been deliberately coached to handle her self-talk and has well rehearsed strategies in place to cope with fear.

On several occasions during the course, Imogen could be heard repeating to herself:

"I'm harnessed so I can't fall. This might be scary, but I can do this".

"Come on Imogen, you've faced tougher things than this. I can't fall so I'm ok".

"It's just the height that makes this scary. These obstacles are actually easy. I can do this".

On several occasions, I heard her cousins say:

"I'm going to fall, I'm going to fall".

"I can't do this, I'm stuck".

Unsurprisingly, for my daughter and her cousins, their self-talk dictated the outcome. Up in the trees and fighting the fear, Imogen demonstrated her ability to manage her state, something which is critical for success whether in sport, relationships or business.

She focused on her permanent strengths ("Come on Imogen, you can get through this, you've faced tougher things than this.")

She avoided paralysis through fear by considering the situation from a variety of angles ("It's just the height that makes this scary. These obstacles are actually easy. I can't fall because I'm harnessed.")

So a key question remains for parents ... how do you teach children to manage their state?

Tip 1 - Be a model:

Children replicate their parent's characteristics. Whatever you want your child to be and whatever you want them NOT to be, examine your own behaviour to check it sets the right example.

You cannot expect your children to manage their state if you're unable to manage yours!

Tip 2 - Zero tolerance to "can't" (for you and your children):

You must be 100% committed to weeding out the word "can't" from their vocabulary (and yours).

Child: "I can't do this."

Parent: "Oh, so you can't do this yet? Let's see what we can do."

Child: "I'll never be able to do this."

Parent: "Ok, you might not be able to do it at the moment, but if we spend some time on it together over the next few weeks, you could do it. What do you think?

The word "can't", leads children to avoid the things which they could conquer in time, and it paralyses them when the pressure is on.

Tip 3 – Coaching approach to parenting

The more you command and the less you coach, the less your children will think for themselves and the less they'll be able to think their way out of difficult situations. Therefore, if you want your children to be successful, you have to encourage them to think for themselves and adopt a coaching/parenting approach instead of a commanding approach:

For example, swap:

Get off the fence because you'll break it. (command)

With:

What will happen if you keep playing on the fence? (coaching)

Allow your children to find the answers for themselves, guiding them to the answers if necessary.

Tip 4 – Strength finding

Invest time with your children to help them discover and remember their unique strengths. Their awareness of the things which make them special and valued will be vital to keeping them positive and logical when they're scared or feeling overwhelmed.

The above case study was written by Andrew Pain for the Impress Coaching Blog, (www.impresscoaching.co.uk/parents-impress-2/)

Ignore them!

Ignoring unwanted behaviour isn't always appropriate when the behaviour is unsafe or unsavoury, however it can be a useful technique to use. It works well because children will often seek any kind of attention, whether it is positive or negative. So ignoring the behaviour you do not like for low level issues, while praising the desired behaviour when it is exhibited can be a very useful technique to help you shape and mould more of the behaviour you want to see and experience. This technique is not an overnight fix and many people give up too soon and claim it doesn't work. However, if you persevere and ensure you use the praise for good behaviour as well as the less responsive reaction to negative behaviour, you will find that unconsciously they soon start to understand the effects of their actions and respond appropriately.

When tests and exams loom near, consider what exercises and activities you can do with children and their friends (group activities) to help reduce the tension levels. When people spend a great deal of time together, a united consciousness can form. (Which is a bit like when you try calling a close friend at the same time as they are calling you!). This means that each student is easily influenced by the thoughts and feeling of their peers, so one person getting nervous or worried can begin to infect the entire group. Ensuring that the children you interact with are getting some "fun" time among the stress can help all students maintain a more balanced state through those challenging few months.

Look for what you want

Some people call it the law of attraction, some say it is caused by the reticular activating system (a part of your brain which works like a radar to pick up on whatever it is that you're looking for or focusing on.) Whatever it is, make sure you look for the results you want. The simple reason is what's known as perception is projection. Whatever you are thinking, however slightly, it will impact upon your behaviour and the messages you are sending out. Not surprisingly, the other person, child or adult, will detect those messages.

Mick's stepson Sean was a fussy eater. His Mom would offer him different foods and would say....."You're probably not going to like this, but......." or she would simply turn her nose up as she offered him something new. No surprises as to what happened! Mick would simply say......."This is something I like – try it and see what you think". Or, he would say......"this is really good for you – how pleased will your Mom be if you eat it all up?" Sean now eats a varied diet and still responds to the offer of small taster bites.

So, think about what responses you expect from the children around you and consider making your expectations more positive. Even if your expectations are not met, it's likely that your response will be a better quality feedback to your child than the "typical, that's exactly what I expected would happen!" approach.

Also, think about how you give feedback to the child in your care. The feedback sandwich encourages you to start with a positive, then move to something of concern and then conclude with another positive. Your influence is heightened because the negative is sandwiched between the positives and the child is more likely to respond.

For example, if a child is having difficulty with spelling, you might first offer praise for the quality of their art work. You could then follow with the news that more attention to detail was required in the spelling of some basic words, then conclude the feedback sandwich by congratulating the child on their imaginative story telling. In so doing, the need to work on spelling is clearly identified, yet in a way that allows the child to remain positive about their skills in general.

Draw away the problems

Do not underestimate the power of drawing. Drawing can be used to personify problems, by turning them into gremlins or monsters. Once you have a character on paper, you can begin to make adjustments to their power level. One little girl Jon knew drew a monster for him that lived under her bed and made her want to go and sleep in her parents room each night. As soon as Jon saw the monster, he recognised him as one that in fact is a "guard monster," who sleeps there to watch over her and protect her through the night. Once he told her this, she was fine.

Remember what we said about the "worry box" too. Committing thoughts and pictures to paper can be a powerful tool for reducing their hold on children.

Case Study #2   How to build confidence in children

Taking the drama out of a crisis

My eldest daughter (aged 11), was brimming with confidence that she'd get a main part in the school play. Given her dramatic skills and the fact that she goes to a private drama academy, she was sure she'd sail through her auditions.

Unfortunately, she didn't secure a main part, or even a small part and was put in the chorus group! She was devastated and it was clear that in spite of her learned resilience, on this occasion, her positive strategies had gone out the window and she'd become stuck in doom and gloom.

"I'm rubbish at drama ... I can't believe I didn't even get one line ... it's not fair ... Why do I even bother going to drama academy?"

It was also clear that we'd need to work through some basic steps to get her back on track and help her to regroup.

Step 1:   Express negative feelings in temporary language

When you're facing defeat, use temporary words like today, at the moment and right now when you express your negative feelings. This helps you to perceive your problems as temporary and if you believe them to be temporary, it feels less overwhelming whether you're an adult or a child. As a result you're more likely to take a positive view of your world, in spite of the problems you face.

So........"I'm gutted at the moment that I didn't get the role I wanted".

Step 2:   Re-enforce your belief that you're a permanently brilliant person

Deliberately emphasise your permanent qualities and indicate that on a different day, it could have been a different result.

"I'm gutted at the moment that I didn't get the role I wanted because I know I'm really good at drama".

Step 3: **Identify the external things which impacted the event**

In the example of my daughter's audition, when we reflected on the external circumstances of the day, we remembered that she almost stayed at home because she was feeling unwell. In the end it was a 50/50 decision and because we were short on child-care options, she went to school, but she was definitely not herself. Try this instead – "I'm gutted at the moment that I didn't get the role I wanted because I know I'm really good at drama. It didn't help that on the day of the auditions that I was feeling unwell and this probably affected my performance in the auditions".

Step 4: **Examine what went wrong and create some learning points**

Finding external factors does not have to be another word for making excuses - so long as you also identify specific learning points to help you improve your performance for next time. In this example, she recognised that because she was feeling unwell, she might not have put as much energy and focus into the audition. Therefore, even though she has a natural flair for drama and should have had the upper hand as a result of her involvement with the drama academy, she needs to ensure that whenever it's time to perform, whether it's drama auditions or something else, she has to give 100%. Anything less and she won't achieve what she wants. When she worked through this learning point, she vowed that next time, she'd be ready - well or unwell!

And so – "I'm gutted at the moment that I didn't get the role I wanted because I know I'm really good at drama. It didn't help that on the day of the auditions, I was feeling unwell and this probably affected my performance in the auditions. I need to ensure that in future, when I perform, I'm fully focused and give 100%".

Step 5: Find something to be grateful for

Highlighting a specific learning point from a set-back is in itself something to be grateful for and working to identify other things for which you can be thankful is a powerful exercise. On this occasion, she felt grateful that in two weeks time, she'd be running the 400M on her school sports day in the gifted and talented section so she had another chance to shine. And so:

"I'm gutted at the moment that I didn't get the role I wanted because I know I'm really good at drama. It didn't help that on the day of the auditions, I was feeling unwell and this probably affected my performance in the auditions. I need to ensure that in future, when I perform, I am fully focused and give 100%. At least I have another chance to make an impact in two weeks time on sports day and I'll ensure I'm completely prepared".

She quickly felt at peace about her disappointment and accepted it. She performed her chorus part with enthusiasm and was gracious about the other children who were given the main roles she so badly wanted and when it came to her 400M on sports day two weeks later, she nailed it and won the race with a gutsy and tactically brilliant run.

The above case study was written by Andrew Pain for the Impress Coaching Blog, (www.impresscoaching.co.uk/parents-impress-2/)

Do something nice

Ask a number of children to write down on a piece of paper something they'd like someone else to do as a favour or treat with their name at the bottom and then put the papers in a hat. Then draw out a name with their favour on and negotiate a day to do that thing with them. In the classroom children could be encouraged to ask for things such as "help tidy my desk" or "learn my French verbs with me." Not only does it encourage giving and gratitude, it also can help new relationships to form.

We wanna be together

When you're spending time with children, really be with them. Jon spent some time with a young lad and asked him to think and behave as if he were his Dad. During one of his answers he put his hand up to signal Jon to pause, while he answered an imaginary mobile phone. Jon had to ask "Dad" to put the phone down and tell him that his phone should be switched off! After the conversation Jon asked the boy what one thing he would change if he could and he said "I'd like Dad to spend more time with me when we are together." Being in the same room as your child clearly isn't the same as giving them your undivided time and energy.

As adults we spend so much of our time thinking and planning for the future. Kids love the here and now – get into the present with them and see how much more you can add to your relationship and how much more fun you can have as a result.

What if??

What if you could pass all of your exams? What would it be like if you could deal with your anger appropriately? Using the "what if" frame of mind can be very powerful with children. It turns the focus to achieving and has the brain imagining the positive end result, which in turn helps the child experience these new results - the unconscious mind will do the rest.

Use your senses

We receive all information from the world through our 5 basic senses - what we see, hear, feel, taste and smell. We then use our senses to form internal representations of our experiences, which is why 2 people who have seen the same event often recall it differently. This is because each of us has one or more preferences for one or more of the senses; some of us are highly visual; some respond to touch or feelings; some are particularly in tune with what they hear and others might have a combination on several senses which can build together as a logical, systematic analysis oft he world.

For example, you may have heard the phrase that...."a picture paints a thousand words". That's extremely true, at least for people who like to see the world in pictures, which is about 25% of us. The people who love to read and hear the words in their mind just got switched off by a simple picture that they don't get.

Communication is about using a range of senses to express ourselves for the benefit of our audience, whoever that may be. So, finding out which of the senses a child predominantly uses is extremely useful when communicating with them – more in the next section.

Case study #3: Nightmares

Jon worked with a young boy, Nathan, who was staying at one of the children's homes. He had a recurring nightmare. In the dream, a skeleton was chasing him and trying to bite him. The dream was very real and frightening to him and he mentioned it several times in therapy sessions with Jon.

Jon found out that Nathan had a 2 feet tall skeleton hanging on his bedroom wall and that he liked to play pretend battle games, with good defeating evil. Jon had the skeleton taken down and asked Nathan's carers to introduce less violent games into his play routine. Then Jon asked Nathan to imagine the skeleton from his dream and the scary stuff that happened. As Nathan pictured this, he felt uneasy, so Jon asked Nathan to give the skeleton a big red hat and big clown sunglasses. As Nathan imagined the picture, his mood lightened a little, so Jon gave the skeleton pink spots on his face and body – just to add to the mix, Jon gave the skeleton the friendly woof of a big, daft dog, as Nathan laughed and enjoyed his new thoughts and feelings.

Nathan's favourite film star was Harry Potter, so Jon then asked Nathan to picture himself as the young wizard, emphasising the colour of the cape, the noisy spells and the size and texture of the wand to make the images, sounds and feelings more intense. Then Jon gave Nathan magic powers to fend off baddies, which included skeletons. Jon told Nathan that whenever he encountered the skeleton, he would find it funny that it had a big red hat and huge clown sunglasses on while woofing like a dog. And the skeleton would turn into a tiny friendly dog as soon as Nathan became Harry Potter and he would know that the skeleton was no longer a threat.

A little while later Jon asked Nathan about the skeleton and he started to laugh and jumped up to zap it with his imaginary wand. The nightmare never returned.

Actions speak louder

You know that old saying "actions speak louder than words?" Well it's true. If there's something you want your child to do, it's no good instructing them from your armchair. You need to get up and show them how to do it and then lead them through their efforts. All people learn in different ways: some people like to understand why they need to do something; some just want to know what it is they need to do; some need to experience a hands-on, practical approach, while others need to think about alternatives – what if we did it this way? Kids are the same.

Remember too that we process information through our senses – what we can see, hear, feel, taste and smell. We all have preferences for one or more of these senses, so that some people understand the world in pictures; they can see what you're talking about, or have a clear vision of the future, while the language they use will reflect their visual preference. Some people need to feel their way – they are quickly in touch, they know when things are uncomfortable. Others like to listen attentively – that doesn't sound right to me, while that's as clear as a bell. Some people like to have a combination of senses, they want it all to make sense, to add up so that they can have a valid opinion. Listen to the words and phrases your kids use – they will tell you what their preferences are. They may be highly visual and need to take a hands-on approach. Or they may be highly thoughtful and will want to know why this is important. They may like to listen and simply need you to tell them clearly what needs to be done. Every combination is possible and by being really present and attentive, you can find the best approach for the kids you live and work with.

Use the skills of someone who can

If a child is unsure about how to do something, ask them if they know someone else who can do it. When they have thought of someone, get them to attempt the activity again while pretending to be the person they know who is already able to do it. This will often lead to an improvement in results and an increase in confidence. This is no more than we routinely do all of our lives. It's how we learned to walk and talk, how we learned to drive, how we learned to behave in our first job – you learn by watching and listening to someone who knows how. When you're really competent, you can develop your own way.

Focus on what you want

Always focus on what you do want, instead of what you don't. So if you want a grumpy teenager to tidy their room, it's not helpful to say, "Your room is a total mess, why can't you be bothered to sort out that dump?" This is because firstly you are drawing attention to the mess when what you really want them to do is to think about being tidy. Also, the question asked is only going to give you all the reasons they've already made up as to why they can't be bothered to tidy their room.

Use this instead............"Your room is not looking tidy and I want it cleaned up please." You may not get too far with that, although it's better than entering into an argument. Then say.............."When will you be tidying your room, before or after dinner?" This gives them the opportunity to think of the room being tidy and also makes the assumption that the room will be tidied – they only have the choice of when. It's really important to give them a choice, rather than an ultimatum. Children often want to feel in control of a situation. If you want them to do a task, and they will not do it because it is not on their terms, give them a choice!........."do you want to get in the bath now or in 5 minutes time?" Either way they will be going in the bath; this way they will feel that it's on their terms as they have made the choice.

And sleeeeeep!

Children often find bedtimes difficult and sometimes can't sleep. This could be due to a number of issues like problems at school or fall outs with friends. These problems build up in their mind and stop them from relaxing into sleep. It's very helpful to have the child write down or draw what's in their head before bed. Another helpful tip is to have the child visualise a blackboard and have them imagine writing their issues on it - then rub the problems out leaving a clear blackboard.

Anchor positive behaviour

When a child shows positive behaviour give them a positive appropriate touch, either on their hand or on their shoulder. Touch them (in the same place) every time they show the positive behaviour and you create what's called a 'resource anchor'. Then when the child is feeling down or showing negative emotions – touch their anchor and watch their behaviour change.

Physical contact between adults and children is an understandably difficult subject. When you have a close personal or family relationship, then the issue is usually more relaxed and physical contact will often be frequent and appropriate. When a professional relationship between adult and child is present, the level of physical contact must be carefully monitored and limited only to that which is necessary. In such a professional relationship, any physical contact must be with the prior approval of any parent or guardian. As such, we believe that a reassuring hand on the shoulder (which may also be the trigger for a powerful resource anchor) is appropriate in most circumstances.

You can do this verbally too. When a child is grumpy or a little tired and there are still things to do, simply ask them to remember a time when they were really happy, or really energetic. As they recall those occasions, ask them to make a great big colourful picture, with lots of movement and sound and to notice how good they feel inside.

Eye movements

There's a lot of information out there about eye accessing cues. Put simply, we all know that our eyes move about as we think, feel and listen to the world. The theory is that closely observing another person's eye movements can give you additional information about their honesty, their character or their preferred way of thinking. Some of that may be true. What we know is that the level of concentration you need to make these most minute of observations is unlikely to be available to you when looking after children!

So, we've come up with a simple version that we can all follow. In simple terms, when a person looks up they are seeing pictures. This may be pictures they've seen before or pictures they've made up. When someone looks to the left or right on the horizontal plain, they're usually hearing sounds – again, either sounds they've heard before or new ones they've just invented. Finally, when looking down, most people are going to their feelings, which could also be the feeling of having a chat with yourself.

So – up = pictures. Sideways = sounds. Down = feelings.

So what's the point? Well, it can be really helpful to know how your child recalls things. For example, if you ask "how was school today?" and they look upwards, you know they're probably thinking of a picture. Next time you ask about a memory, help them to recall it by saying....."when you think of your holiday, what do you see?" Remember the old story of a teacher who asked a child a question in class, only for the stumbling child to look upwards. The teacher booms...."The answer isn't on the ceiling!"........ although, truth is, for that child it may well have been.

A big health warning here. Eye movements can never be reliably used for judging whether people are being honest with you. Especially children, who are encouraged to use make-believe all the time. Use eye movements to better understand your children and to help them be more vivid in their descriptions.

Case study #4:   The Dentist!

Mick's stepson Sean needed extensive dental work to realign his teeth, something Mick himself should have had done as a child, but was too frightened to. So when Sean got upset and worried before the treatment started, Mick had first hand memories of the terror Sean was feeling.

When they talked about it, Mick asked what the worst part was. Sean described this over-bearing consultant getting really close and barking at him in an unfriendly manner, while instruments were sticking in his mouth. As Sean talked he got anxious and it was apparent that the most significant part of his fear was the sound of the man's harsh voice. So, Mick asked Sean to imagine the dentist talking like Donald Duck. As Sean visibly relaxed, he smiled and opened his eyes. As he did so, Mick asked him to change the dentist's face to that of Donald Duck too. Big smile now! As Sean relaxed more, Mick asked him to make a picture of the surgery, looking at himself in the chair, being treated by Donald Duck. As Sean looked at the picture in his mind's eye, Mick told him to shrink it down, until it was smaller than a postage stamp stuck on his little toe.

A few days later Sean had the first of 4 extractions, then had his brace fitted and went back for regular adjustments over the next 2 years. He never shed a tear.

The power of story-telling

Story telling is an age old past-time enjoyed by millions of people of all ages. It can also be extremely therapeutic in helping the listener to move from one not-so-good emotional state to another, preferred state. For this to be done successfully, the story needs to be logical and should match the listener's experience – the plot then takes the listener from where they are to where the storyteller wants them to be. Along the way, the listener's unconscious mind will be trying to make sense of the messages and relate them to their own world.

So, here's an example – a traditional children's story for little ones.

Little Nicky:

Little Nicky was a wonderful red squirrel who had big blue eyes and a huge fluffy long tail. He was beautiful. He had the ability to be busy doing something all of the time; he was into everything, gathering nuts and food from all of the trees and hiding them in lots of different places. This ability protected him from any enemies that he might meet in the woods, so they wouldn't steal his food. But because Little Nicky was hardly ever still he never stopped moving long enough to see all of the amazing colours of the woods where he lived and all of the other different animals that lived there with him.

This made him sad and when he heard other squirrels telling stories of slowing down to see the changes in the woods due to the different seasons, he felt even sadder. They talked about how peaceful and calming it can be to watch the world go by. Little Nicky missed all of this, but no matter how hard he tried, he just could not keep still.

One day he found himself not being able to remember where he had hidden his stash of food. He became hungry and angry. As he started to trace his thoughts he remembered what the other squirrels were talking about. About how peaceful and calming the woods can be; as he remembered these thoughts he noticed that his little paws began to relax. He was delighted with this discovery and decided to see if this would work again. He closed his eyes and pictured the woods being calm and peaceful. He noticed the stillness of the magnificent trees. Again his body began to slow down and relax. Because of this he could remember where he had hidden his food!

Little Nicky was so pleased and he shared his new thoughts with other squirrels who really enjoyed listening to him. The other squirrels welcomed Nicky into their circle of friends so that they could play and learn together.

A really short story about an appealing creature who is busy being busy, so much so that he misses out on other things and important friendships along the way; by listening and learning from others, he improves his life and gets more enjoyment from a different perspective. Easier than telling a busy child to slow down and smell the roses!

Our unconscious minds enjoy stories and often can be influenced by images, pictures and symbols. In ordinary conversation, we often use the phrase....."a friend of mine........" as an introduction to a story. This is the 'my friend John' routine and it works brilliantly with children and adolescents alike. Never under-estimate the power of a good story – and never be concerned about embellishing it to make it even more interesting and powerful!

The authors

Jonathan Martin is a hypnotherapist, psychotherapist and master practitioner of NLP. His studies have lasted over 15 years, during which time he has worked extensively with extremely disadvantaged children in care homes, helping to produce some incredible life stories. He is now responsible for the therapeutic treatment of children in care, while he also finds time to offer therapy to adults with a wide range of concerns. Married, he is the proud father of Layla Mai.

Mick Rose is a trainer and coach, a master practitioner and trainer of NLP and a hypnotherapist. Also married, he has several children and grand-children and has been involved in senior management and performance delivery in both the public and private sectors. Now semi-retired, he enjoys doing as little as possible.

The reason for this collaboration is that they both have something to offer those who are looking after children. This is not a book about parenting – it is relevant for child-minders, baby-sitters, parents, grandparents, neighbours, teachers, dinner ladies, aunts and uncles – in short, anyone who might look after a child for a period of time, however short.

The book is easy to understand and written in plain English because these are simple techniques that make a difference. There is no need to feel helpless or clueless – just try these methods for yourself. If you don't feel more resourceful as a result – they will give you your money back.

(C) Hednesford Publications 2014

Printed in Great Britain
by Amazon